Workbook of Reflections, Creativity, Dreams, and Imaginations!

Roberta McGill

gatekeeper press™
Columbus, OH

Abella and the Magical Afro Puffs Workbook of Reflections, Creativity, Dreams, and Imaginations!

Published by Gatekeeper Press
2167 Stringtown Rd, Suite 109
Columbus, OH 43123-2989
www.GatekeeperPress.com

ISBN (paperback): 9781662914553

INTRODUCTION

Abella and the Magical Afro Puffs is the story of a young girl who discovered that she had magic hair. She learned that her two afro puffs were able to transport her to different, magical places, places outside of her daily travel. These magical afro puffs were Abella's unique quality. Although Abella is a fictional character, we all have something unique to us.

The purpose of this workbook is to stretch your imagination and to help you explore and learn more about yourself and what is important to you. It's designed to help you reflect on things you may not have thought about before. Think about things outside of your comfort zone. What are your unique qualities? How can you make a difference?

1.

Unique - the only one of its kind unlike anything else.
What is unique about you? Fill the pages with your unique qualities.

2.

Imagine you have a superpower. What would it be and how would you use it? Would it help others?

3.

NAME THREE THINGS YOU LIKE ABOUT YOURSELF. WHY DID YOU CHOOSE THEM? WAS THIS DIFFICULT FOR YOU? OR WAS IT EASY? REFLECT ON WHY.

4.

Let's be creative and think outside the box. Make your own language. Write a sentence. What does it say?

5.

If you had to plan a party, what kind would it be? (for example, a tea party, a dinner party, a dance party).

Who would you invite?

What activities would you have and why? (eating cookie dough, dancing, sky diving, painting, etc.)

6.

DRAW A PICTURE THAT MAKES YOU SMILE. REFLECT ON WHY IT MAKES YOU SMILE.

7.

If you could invent something, what would it be? Why is it important to you?

8.

What do you want to be when you grow up? Why?

9.

What makes you proud?

10.

Draw a page with patterns. What do you like about it? Why did you choose this pattern?

11.

Fill the pages with as many positive words as you can think of. How many apply to you (hopefully all)?

CONCLUSION

Now that you have had the opportunity to reflect, create, dream and imagine, it's time to act! What can you do to make a difference? Below are some ideas. I am sure you can think of more ideas.

- Give someone a compliment
- Smile at someone
- Write a nice note to your teacher or a friend
- Collect socks for a shelter
- Do a chore for your sibling
- Schedule a ZOOM dance party
- Pick up trash in your neighborhood
- Draw a picture and give it to someone to make them smile
- Write a letter to your local representative about a cause that it important to you
- Bake cookies for someone
- Tell someone a funny story
- Share your favorite memory with your parent
- Donate clothes that you have outgrown to an organization
- Read a story to someone young
- Volunteer to an organization
- Send cards to residents at an older adult facility
- Make or buy dinner for a neighbor
- Start a club (book club, writing club, poetry club)

www.ingramcontent.com/pod-product-compliance
Lightning Source LLC
Chambersburg PA
CBHW040246070526
44654CB00059B/1817